JULIETTE LOW: GIRL SCOUT FOUNDER
is the story of a warm, friendly
woman who had a great desire
"to be useful and to help others."
Throughout her life, Daisy Low
tried to live up to the Promise and
Laws of the organization she
founded. She not only worked for
American girls, but for Scouting
and Guiding all over the world.
Because of her efforts, every
Scout can truly become "a friend
to all and a sister to every other
Girl Scout."

GARRARD PUBLISHING COMPANY
CHAMPAIGN, ILLINOIS

Juliette
Low

GIRL SCOUT FOUNDER

by Ruby L. Radford

illustrated by Vic Dowd

j B
L95n

This book is for
Kathryn Dixon Bishop

The author and publisher are grateful to
Pennsylvania Military College
for permission to quote the first stanza of "Taps."

Contents

1. Home Again 7
2. Summers at the Cliffs 13
3. School Days 21
4. Daisy Marries 27
5. "Little Stars that Guide" . . . 35
6. Daisy's First Girl Guides . . . 41
7. Something Wonderful
   for America 48
8. Girl Scouts Serve America . . . 56
9. Camp Juliette Low 65
10. For All the World 73

1

Home Again

Daisy ran to the top of the curving stairs. Her taffy-colored pigtails were flying, her brown eyes bright. Her older sister, Nellie, and her little sister, Alice, ran laughing behind her.

Daisy threw her leg over the banister. Squealing with delight, she slid to the lower hall. At the bottom two strong arms caught her.

"How good it is to have my three little girls home again," said Mr. Gordon, as he hugged them.

Daisy looked up into his handsome face and asked, "Papa, you won't ever go off and leave us again, will you?"

Daisy was only five years old. For most of her life, her father had been away fighting for the South in the Civil War.

"The war is over," Mr. Gordon told Daisy. "Now we can all stay together again."

That very day he had brought his wife and three little daughters home to Savannah, Georgia. They had spent eight months in Chicago with Grandmother Juliette Kinzie after the Northern soldiers had captured Savannah.

Daisy loved the people of the North, who had been so kind to them. She could not understand why the North and South had fought. "I hate war," Daisy told her father. "I want everybody to be friends."

The Gordon family was grateful that their beautiful home had not been burned by Northern soldiers. Daisy had been born there on October 31, 1860. She was named Juliette, for Grandmother Kinzie, but everyone called her Daisy.

Now Daisy and her sisters explored the house again. They ran out to see the roses and camellia bushes. They climbed their favorite tree in the middle of the garden. Each girl had a limb for her playhouse.

"I'm glad the soldiers didn't cut down this tree for firewood," said Nellie.

Daisy was sitting in the tree when she heard a cat meow. She jumped down, and a skinny gray kitten rubbed against her stocking.

"You look starved, poor kitty," said Daisy.

She gave him some milk, and made a bed for him in the empty carriage house. There had been little food for animals during the war. It was not long before Daisy added a lame duck and a hungry puppy to her pets.

The Gordon girls played with their many cousins too. Meta, Randy and Elise Anderson lived nearby. They rigged up a line between the two houses. They had a wheel at each end of the line. They turned the wheel to pull messages back and forth.

One afternoon they made taffy. The
cane syrup was boiled on a wood-burning
stove. When it cooled a little, they pulled
it.

Randy said, "Look! This candy is just
the color of Daisy's hair. Let's braid
them together."

Daisy was always game for anything.
Too late the children saw their mistake.

The candy had hardened and would not come out of Daisy's hair. Mrs. Gordon was very angry. She scolded Daisy while she tried to get it out. Finally Daisy's beautiful hair had to be cut off.

Daisy did not worry about her short hair. She was too happy to be back home with her friends and Grandma Gordon.

Every afternoon Grandma invited Daisy and Nellie to her room for tea. Daisy liked the tea and cookies. She tried hard not to break any of Grandma's fine china.

On Sunday afternoons Mrs. Gordon taught them the catechism. Daisy wished she could read the Bible stories herself.

"Next fall you can learn to read," her mother promised. "We will let you go to school with Nellie."

Daisy thought fall would never come.

2

Summers at the Cliffs

Daisy's first teacher was Miss Lucille Blois. Miss Lucille had a school in her own home. It was only a short walk from Daisy's house.

Daisy liked drawing best of all her lessons. Spelling and arithmetic were very hard for her.

Red-haired Bill, Daisy's first brother, was born the year she started to school.

Later there were Mabel and baby Arthur. Daisy and Nellie helped look after the younger children.

The summer Daisy was nine, yellow fever broke out in Savannah. Many people died. Mr. Gordon said to his wife, "I think we should send the children to their Aunt Eliza Stiles."

Mrs. Gordon agreed. "It's cooler in north Georgia. There is no yellow fever at Etowah Cliffs."

Daisy and Nellie could hardly wait for the train to reach their aunt's home.

The big house was on a cliff above the river. Uncle George's four boys came also. Sometimes there were 20 children. The girls slept in beds. The boys had to sleep on mattresses on the floor, but they didn't mind.

There was a goat cart to ride in, and
many animals. Peaches, pears, cherries,
apples and figs ripened in the orchard.
In the attic was a trunk where the
children kept cast-off finery of their
parents. These were costumes for their
plays.

Daisy was always a leader. She made up plays. She could sing, dance and recite well. She told the children about her great-grandmother, in the North, who was captured by Seneca Indians when she was nine years old. For four years she was a princess in the tribe. The Indians called her "Little-Ship-Under-Full-Sail" because she could run so fast. When her parents finally found her, the girl rushed into her mother's arms. The chief's heart was softened, and he let her go home.

"Let's make it into a play," said Daisy. "I want to be Little-Ship."

The other girls were Indian squaws. The boys were warriors. They made warbonnets, bows and arrows. They painted their faces with pokeberry juice.

The cousins met every summer at Etowah Cliffs. One year they decided to publish a magazine. Every child had to write something for it. Daisy drew the pictures. She also wrote stories and poems. Once she wrote a poem that began:

"*I was passing by a pig-sty,*
When I heard a piggy say,
'*I would rather live in rubbish*
Forever and a day.'"

Some of the grownups didn't like the poems. So Daisy explained to them, "I get tired of reading goody-goody poems and stories all the time."

On hot days the children swam in the river. Sometimes they pretended the cliff above the river was their castle. The cliff was the scene of many good times.

Mockingbirds, cardinals and brown thrashers sang in the tall pines. Daisy learned their songs. When a baby bird fell from the nest she climbed the tree to put it back. She hunted wild flowers, gooseberries and scuppernong grapes in the woods.

When the boys caught fish they had a fish fry on the rocks below the castle. Later around the campfire they sang Stephen Foster songs. But best of all they liked the song *Dixie*. When the fire died down, they watched the stars and learned many of their names.

Daisy was always sad when fall came and she had to go back to Savannah. But she took home many happy memories.

3

School Days

When Daisy was thirteen she and Nellie were sent to boarding school in Virginia. Stuart Hall was run by the Misses Randolph. They were the granddaughters of Thomas Jefferson, author of the Declaration of Independence.

Daisy wrote often to her parents. She reported honestly about her lessons and conduct. She still liked drawing and painting best. Spelling was as hard as ever. Once her mother sent her a list of words she had misspelled in her letter.

Daisy wrote back, *"A dictionary is no use—half the time I don't know how the word starts!"*

Daisy still loved pets. She wrote her mother, *"We found a little robin frozen to death and gave it a burial next day at recess."*

In another letter she confessed, *"Mama, I can't keep all the rules. I'm too much like you . . . I'll keep clear of big scrapes, but little ones I can't avoid."*

When Daisy was home on winter vacation, she saw some ragged children at a fruit stand. She told her friends about them.

"Let's start a sewing club and make them some clothes," Daisy said.

"That's a good idea," one of the girls agreed.

"We'll call our club 'The Helpful Hands,'" Daisy decided.

"But, Daisy," said another friend, "we don't know how to sew."

Daisy did not know how to sew either. But she learned and tried to teach the others. At their first meeting, The Helpful Hands were learning to thread needles. Daisy got mixed up and taught the girls to thread their needles with their left hands.

When the Gordon boys heard about this, they teased their sister.

"Helpful Hands!" Bill laughed. "You should be called 'The Helpless Hands'!"

This didn't bother Daisy. The girls all soon learned to sew. They had a good time at their meetings. And they felt that they were doing something useful for others.

After two years at Stuart Hall, Daisy went to Edge Hill School, also in Virginia. Daisy was becoming a fine artist. She drew pictures of the kinds of dresses she wanted, and sent the drawings home. Her mother used them when she went shopping for Daisy's new clothes.

Next Daisy went to a school in New York City. It was run by two French ladies who were very strict. The girls spoke nothing but French and dressed like French schoolgirls. They wore long black aprons over their dresses. The girls were not allowed on the street alone. A teacher marched them, two by two, up Madison Avenue for exercise.

Daisy disliked the rules, but she loved her painting lessons. She studied with a well-known artist.

The next year Mrs. Gordon decided that Alice should go to school with Daisy. Alice didn't want to leave Edge Hill, but Daisy begged her to come. "I'm lonesome without one of my sisters," she said.

So Alice went with Daisy to New York. Early in December Alice became ill with scarlet fever. Mrs. Gordon came north to nurse her, and Alice was better for a while. Then suddenly she became worse and died soon after Christmas. Daisy was heartbroken. She partly blamed herself for begging Alice to come with her.

4
Daisy Marries

"Now that you are almost twenty-two," Mr. Gordon said when Daisy finished school, "I want you to have a trip abroad."

"Oh, Papa!" cried Daisy joyously. "Then I can visit the Lows in England. The girls invite me every time they leave Savannah. How wonderful!"

"But mind you," her father warned, "I don't want you to get interested in that young Willy Low. All he thinks of is spending his father's money."

"Why, Papa, I hardly know him. He's usually traveling when his sisters are in Savannah."

Daisy pretended to be surprised, but secretly she thought Willy Low a real Prince Charming. He was tall, with blond hair and blue eyes. He was the most fascinating man she had ever met.

The Low family often came from England to their beautiful home on Lafayette Square in Savannah. The old millionaire, Andrew Low, had business interests in Georgia.

During that summer of sight-seeing, Daisy did fall in love with Willy Low. On December 21, 1886, she and Willy were married at Christ Church in Savannah. Daisy became Juliette Gordon Low.

After the reception the couple was showered with rice. A grain fell in one of Daisy's ears and damaged her eardrum. After the rice was removed, Daisy discovered she was deaf in that ear. An abscess had already dulled the hearing in her other ear. She knew she would never be able to hear well. But Daisy tried not to let it bother her.

Daisy and Willy lived in Savannah for a while. Then they went to England, where Willy rented a house near his old home. Three years later he bought Wellsbourne, a beautiful estate with gardens and stables for their horses. Each summer they went to the Scottish highlands for hunting and fishing.

Willy and Daisy had many friends among the nobility and led a gay life.

They went to dinner parties and dances, to operas and plays. Once Daisy danced with the Prince of Wales, who became Edward VII, King of England. She was presented at Court to Queen Victoria.

Daisy and Willy gave many parties. Daisy's guests always had a good time.

"Mrs. Low," one of her guests said, "you serve the most delicious food I have ever eaten. What is your secret?"

Daisy laughed gaily. "It's American cooking! I brought my cook, Mosianna Milledge, from Savannah. No one can bake hickory-cured ham and candied potatoes like Mosianna."

Daisy's sister Mabel often came for long visits. Finally she married an Englishman named Rowland Leigh, and lived in England.

After one of Daisy's gay dinners, Mabel said, "Daisy, you were the life of the party. How do you do it?"

Daisy smiled. "I don't hear half they say, so the best thing is to take over and amuse them." Daisy's hearing was growing worse.

Daisy often traveled abroad. She and Willy went to Egypt once and saw the Pyramids. This was the only time they went abroad together. Willy liked to go to the jungles of Africa and India to hunt lions and elephants. While he was away, Daisy traveled about with friends.

Daisy made friends in many foreign countries. Her sympathies were stirred by poor and uneducated people in many primitive places. She always wanted to help them.

Once, in England, she met a poor woman whose husband had deserted her. The woman needed to earn money to support her children.

"I'm going to America," said Daisy. "Come with me. I'll find work for you."

Daisy not only found the woman a job, she also brought the woman's children to the United States. Daisy could never see a human or an animal in need without trying to help. Since she traveled a great deal and met many kinds of people, her sympathies soon encircled the world.

5

"Little Stars that Guide"

The train chugged into Savannah.

"Aunt Daisy's coming home!" cried Arthur, Jr. He was waiting beside the tracks.

Daisy stepped off the train with her Pekingese dog and a pet mockingbird in a cage. Bella, the Scottish maid, followed with Polly Poons, the parrot. Daisy's parents and some of their grandchildren welcomed her warmly.

After a big supper at the Gordon home, Daisy's nephews and nieces wanted to see what their aunt had brought them. Little Eleanor, Nellie's daughter, loved the smell of leather and French soap when the trunks were opened. Arthur, Jr., was thrilled with books about camels and sheiks and how they lived in the deserts of Africa.

Later, Daisy's namesake, little Daisy Doots, begged for a story. The children laughed in delight as they listened. No one could tell funnier tales than Aunt Daisy.

Daisy went back to Savannah as often as she could. When she was in England she was often lonely. She had no children, and her husband was often away.

To pass the days, Daisy copied a painting of her mother. She carved a mantel for the fireplace. She hammered out a pair of iron gates for Wellsbourne.

Every week she visited a sick neighbor. "You are the kindest, best friend I have," said the old lady. Daisy had taken her some cakes and read to her from the Bible. "No one else comes to see me."

Daisy didn't tell her that people thought she had leprosy and were afraid they would catch it. But Daisy wasn't afraid. She knew how it felt to be lonely.

In 1905 Daisy's husband died. Her beloved family was her greatest comfort then. Later Daisy tried to take up her old life. She traveled to India, but she was restless and unhappy. She worked harder at her art, but she still felt empty.

Then something happened that changed Daisy's whole life. At a luncheon she met General Sir Robert Baden-Powell. Daisy wrote her father about him. *"He is a genius as a soldier and he draws, paints and models as well. He left the army against King Edward's wishes . . . to organize the Boy Scouts and now he has forty thousand boys all over Great Britain, with branches in the U.S.A., France and Germany."*

Daisy met Sir Robert several times. He often talked about his work with the Boy Scouts. Daisy began to feel his enthusiasm. She thought back over her life. It had been filled with fun and travel. But she had not been very useful.

"I feel like my life has been wasted," she told Sir Robert.

He replied kindly, *"There are little stars that guide us on, although we do not realize it."*

Sir Robert's sister, Agnes, had started Girl Guide companies, or troops, for girls who wanted to do Scout work. Daisy went to their meetings in London and visited their camps.

She invited Sir Robert and his sister to visit her in Scotland. They helped her make plans to organize a company for Scottish girls. Daisy was delighted that at last she had found something to do that would help others.

6

Daisy's First
Girl Guides

Daisy opened the door at Lochs, her
home in the mountains of Scotland.

"Are you Mrs. Low?" asked a golden-
haired girl about twelve years old.

"Yes, my dear. Come right in," said
Daisy.

"I'm late, but I had to walk six miles,"
said the girl. "I came to your meeting."

Daisy led the way into a large room
where six other girls were already seated.

Some of the girls had never been in so fine a house. Their homes were simple cottages.

Daisy had invited them to form her first Girl Guide company. She loved girls and knew how to make them feel at ease. She showed them Polly Poons. They giggled when her pet mocking-bird snatched a pen from her hand. Soon they forgot their shyness.

A maid brought in tea and cookies. While they ate, Daisy told them what fun Girl Guides had in London. She told how they worked and played together.

"There'll be merit badges for those who learn special skills," she said.

She picked up a long strip of leather. "Watch. I'll show you right now how to tie a square knot."

The girls were delighted to be Girl Guides. They met with Daisy every week during the summer. They went on bird walks and camping trips. They learned about highland plants and animals, and to cook over campfires. They learned how to signal from hill to hill with flags. Daisy taught them Scottish history, first aid and how to help with housework.

One afternoon a girl of thirteen looked sad. "What's wrong?" asked Daisy.

"My sister, Anne, is going to work in the woolen mill in the city. When I'm older I'll have to leave home too. Our family needs all of the money each of us can earn."

"My cousin went to the city," another girl said softly. "She got sick with a lung disease and died."

"Maybe we can think of some way you can earn money at home. Then you won't have to work in the mills," said Daisy. "Wait! I have an idea! Why can't you raise chickens?"

The girls began to talk excitedly. "We could sell chickens and eggs to the vacationers who come to Scotland every summer and fall."

Daisy knew little about chickens, but she found someone who did. He taught the girls how to raise chickens. Daisy didn't know how to spin wool into thread, either, but she bought a spinning wheel. She learned how to spin and taught her Girl Guides. Now the girls could spin sheep's wool into thread. It brought them more money.

Daisy's Girl Guides enjoyed working

and playing together. Most important, they learned to make better lives for themselves.

When winter came the local post-mistress took charge of the Guides. Daisy went to London and started a company in a rundown part of the city. She rented a basement for the company and brought a basket of food to every meeting. The girls enjoyed playing games, singing and doing handicrafts.

Soon Daisy started a second company in London. She saw how wonderful the work was for girls. It gave them a chance to make friends, learn useful things and become better citizens. Daisy longed to start companies in America.

She asked Mrs. Mark Kerr, whom she scarcely knew, to take charge of her London Guides.

"I don't know anything about girls," Mrs. Kerr replied, "and I have no time."

Daisy pretended she didn't hear. She said brightly, "Then that's settled! Their meeting is Thursday. Be sure to serve a nice tea at every meeting. I'll pay for the tea and other expenses."

Then Daisy left before Mrs. Kerr could refuse again. Soon she sailed for America to start Girl Guide work there.

7

Something Wonderful for America

When Daisy reached Savannah she telephoned her cousin, Nina Pape.

"Come right over," Daisy said excitedly. *"I've got something for the girls of Savannah, and all America, and all the world, and we're going to start it tonight."*

Nina came right over. She agreed that Girl Guiding would be fine for girls.

Later Daisy asked ten other women to help, including her mother.

Young Page Anderson was one of the first girls to be interested. Page was the daughter of Daisy's cousin, Randy Anderson. It was Randy who had braided taffy into Daisy's hair.

"Some friends and I have been camping and studying nature," Page said. "We would like to join the Girl Guides."

Daisy invited Page's group and some other girls to a tea at her parents' home. She told them about Girl Guide work. She showed them pictures of Girl Guides in uniforms around campfires. Many of the girls were eager to become Guides. On March 12, 1912, they formed two patrols, as troops were then called.

"Where will we meet?" asked Page.

"You may use the carriage house on Charlton Street behind my house," said Daisy. "You can play basketball on the vacant lot across the street."

"Will our uniforms be expensive?" asked another girl.

"Oh, no," said Daisy. "We can make them ourselves."

They finally agreed on dark blue skirts and middy blouses with light blue ties.

The girls went on walks and kept notes of all the birds they saw. They learned lifesaving and first aid.

After one first aid class, the patrol members kept their bandages on and went to the home of one of the girls. The girl's mother almost fainted when she saw them. She was certain they had all been in an accident.

Soon there were six patrols in Savannah. They played intertroop basketball in knee-length bloomers. Young girls in those days wore long skirts. It was thought immodest to be seen in bloomers on the street. Canvas curtains were strung around the basketball court. The curtains hid the girls from curious people who went by.

Miss Edith Johnston became secretary of the Savannah Girl Guides. When Daisy returned to England, she gave Miss Johnston the English Girl Guide Handbook. She said, *"It will tell you what you need to know, and if it doesn't, use your common sense."*

Daisy worked with the Girl Guides in England to learn more about their organization. She wanted to know how they trained their leaders. She came back to America eager and full of new ideas. But that autumn her happiness was cut short. Her father, who had cheered and helped her, died in September.

Daisy worked harder than ever for her Girl Guides. Mr. W. J. Hoxie, the naturalist, worked with Daisy to revise the English handbook to suit American girls. They called the book *How Girls Can Help Their Country.*

Daisy wrote to her friends throughout America to interest them in starting patrols. Soon there were groups in many places. The name was changed to Girl Scouts, and patrols were called troops. The new uniforms were khaki instead of dark blue. The blue had showed the dirt when the girls went hiking.

Daisy bought the Savannah Scouts a motorboat. She also bought a camping site outside the city. She took Page Anderson's group on a five-day camping trip. They hiked, swam and went boating. Mr. Hoxie taught them nature lore and how to cook in the open.

54

When camp was over Page said, "It was so much fun we didn't even mind the mosquitoes."

More and more girls in America were joining troops. Daisy met with the President's wife and other important people to talk about making the Girl Scouts a national organization.

Daisy told Edith Johnston, "We're opening a national headquarters. I want you to become national secretary. Headquarters will be in Washington, D. C."

Miss Johnston felt overcome at so much responsibility. She said afterward, *"Yet I could not refuse her. I had seen what Girl Guiding had come to mean to our Savannah girls. . . . I knew what it would mean to girls everywhere if it could be brought to them."*

8
Girl Scouts Serve America

Daisy traveled about America, organizing Girl Scout troops in many cities. She often returned to England to see about her Girl Guides there.

During a visit to Savannah, Daisy presented badges at one of the troop meetings. The girls were proud when their founder stepped onto the platform in her uniform. Then giggles were heard around the room.

"Look!" whispered a girl. "Miss Daisy has brought our badges in an old tomato can! Imagine!"

They could never predict what Miss Daisy would do. That was part of her charm. She was always a girl at heart.

When World War I broke out in 1914, Daisy's income from England was cut off. Until then she had been paying all expenses of the national work herself.

"Now you can't pay the Girl Scout expenses," said her mother.

"I'll sell my pearls to raise the money," said Daisy.

Many people, especially old friends, began sending money to the Washington headquarters. In 1916, National Headquarters was moved from Washington to New York City.

Younger girls wanted to join the Scouts. Daisy told them, "In England the younger girls are called Brownies. They are named after the brownie helpers of the folktales."

In 1916, the first Brownie troop was organized in Marblehead, Massachusetts. Soon Brownies were organized in other cities. Now girls as young as seven could join the Scouting movement.

Their Promise was: *"I promise to do my best to love God and my country, to help other people every day, especially those at home."*

The United States entered World War I in 1917. Soon afterwards Daisy met with all the Girl Scouts in Savannah. "What is our Promise?" she asked.

The older Scouts repeated the Promise:

"On my honor I will try:

To do my duty to God and my country,

To help other people at all times,

To obey the Girl Scout Laws."

"And what is our motto?" Daisy asked.

"Be prepared," the Scouts replied.

"Now is the time to do our duty to God and our country," said Daisy. "In earning your badges you have begun to

prepare yourselves. Now each girl must think of some way she can help to win the war."

"I've learned to drive a car," said an older girl. "I can work in the Red Cross Motor Corps."

"I've earned my sewing badge," said another. "I can help in the sewing room."

Then an eight-year-old Brownie spoke up, "I can take care of my little sister so Mama can do more at home."

Later, Girl Scouts marched in patriotic parades all over America. They sold Liberty Bonds by the thousands to raise money for the war effort.

When the war was over, there were 40,000 Girl Scouts in the United States. Scouting was also spreading to many other lands.

Daisy went back to England in 1919. Lady Baden-Powell, wife of Sir Robert, was now head of the Girl Guides there. She wanted Girl Guides and Girl Scouts to form an International Council.

Daisy thought the idea was a fine one. If girls from all over the world could meet and become friends, perhaps there would be better understanding among countries.

The leaders met to make plans. Girls from many countries came to the first World Camp. It was such a success that World Camps were held every two years.

In 1924, the World Camp was at Foxlease, a beautiful estate in England. Daisy's cottage there was named "The Link," for she was a real link between the girls of England and America.

The cottage had the only bathtub in camp. "Come over any time and get a bath," Daisy invited. Some campers came each morning and often stayed for breakfast.

Daisy had special teas at The Link. Girls from foreign countries talked with her around the cozy living room fire. Daisy's dream of world friendships was at last coming true.

9

Camp Juliette Low

Girl Scout camps were held in many parts of the United States.

Daisy picked out a campsite on the Georgia side of Lookout Mountain. Mr. Ledbetter, the owner, gave the land to the Scouts. Daisy and some other leaders went there to get the papers signed and sealed. They learned that Mr. Ledbetter was high on the mountain working on a road. That didn't stop Daisy.

Her old car was filled with suitcases, her Pekingese dog and her friends. Daisy drove them up the bumpy mountain road. Mr. Ledbetter was working at the top of a cliff.

"Can you climb up?" he shouted to Daisy.

"I can, but my dog can't," she replied.

Somehow she got the pet to the top too. The paper was signed and legally sealed. Then Daisy and her friends looked over the campsite. There was a mountain pool for swimming, beautiful trees and rocks.

"No trees are to be cut," Daisy ordered.

She decided where the dining hall and other buildings would be put up. She was delighted later when the camp was named Camp Juliette Low.

That summer she visited during the camping season. Flags waved as the girls greeted their founder. Daisy was as happy as any of the girls.

They sang gayly to the tune of *Dixie*:
"Away down south in old Savannah,
   First was raised the Girl Scout
      banner,
   Daisy Low, Daisy Low, Daisy Low,
   Founder dear."

Around the campfire, Daisy told the girls ghost stories laid in a castle she had once rented in Scotland. She half-believed these stories herself. Delightful chills ran down the girls' spines.

Daisy's stories and her fortune-telling became famous in all the camps she visited. For fun, she liked to read the girls' palms.

By 1924 there were 100,000 Girl Scouts!

During these busy years Daisy had many personal sorrows. Her mother died. Daisy was now almost totally deaf, and she was not well. After an operation she learned she had cancer.

She continued, however, to go to international meetings in England. In 1925, plans were discussed for the Fourth World Camp. Daisy asked to have it in America. This had been her dream ever since the World Camps started.

"European delegates can't afford such a long trip," she was told.

"Our Girl Scouts will help pay for the trips," Daisy promised.

They argued, but Daisy insisted. She returned to New York full of plans and hurried to the Girl Scout Headquarters.

"*We are going to have the World Camp here next year*," she told Mrs. Jane Rippin, a scout official. "At Camp Edith Macy."

"But the camp is still only woodland," argued Mrs. Rippin. "Not a building has been put up. We can't possibly get it ready in time."

"*Jane*," Daisy said to Mrs. Rippin, "*if we don't have it next year, I won't be here.*"

Then Mrs. Rippin realized how ill Daisy was. She and her co-workers did everything possible to make Daisy's dream of a World Camp in America come true.

In spite of her suffering, Daisy became a whirlwind of activity. Roads were cleared on the camp site in Pleasantville, New York. Wells were dug and pipes laid. A great hall was built of native stone. A number of smaller buildings were put up. By May, 1926, Camp Edith Macy was ready. Under Daisy's leadership the miracle had been performed.

10
For All the World

In May, 1926, a radiant Daisy Low rode into Camp Edith Macy beside Lady Baden-Powell. They led a long line of cars filled with adult Girl Scouts and 56 foreign Girl Guide delegates. They had come from 39 countries to a World Camp in America.

Daisy's heart glowed with happiness when she saw the flags of many countries

waving in the breeze. Dogwood and apple trees were in bloom. Birds sang their welcome. The cars stopped. Daisy stepped out to greet her guests.

"Welcome to Camp Edith Macy," she said as they left the cars. "Look for the flag of your country. The American girl holding it will be your companion and guide while you are in camp."

Later Daisy and Lady Baden-Powell climbed the hill to the Great Hall where supper was served. Log fires crackled in the stone fireplaces at each end of the hall. The flags of all the nations had been placed along the walls.

After supper the visiting Girl Guides brought greetings. Each delegate placed some sticks of her country's native wood on the blazing fire. Each told what her country had to offer the world.

A Japanese delegate in a flowery silk kimono said, *"The land of cherry blossoms brings the art and literature of an ancient civilization."*

Another Girl Guide said, *"From South Africa gold and diamonds I bring."*

When the greetings were over, Daisy remarked to Lady Baden-Powell, *"Scouting and Guiding can be the magic thread which links the youth of the world together."*

"Yes, indeed," agreed her friend. "They have already created many lasting world friendships."

At night Daisy went to bed exhausted and in pain. No one knew except those who shared her living quarters.

In the morning she greeted everyone with a happy smile. She often had breakfast with some of the Scouts or Guides. They often cooked outdoors. After breakfast Daisy told their fortunes.

"I see you will become a great leader," she said to an English Girl Guide.

Some took her words so seriously they worked hard to make them come true. Daisy was among her Girl Scouts and Girl Guides as much as possible. They talked about their troops back home. Daisy delighted them with her funny experiences. She embraced the whole camp with her love. It was one of the happiest weeks of her life.

Daisy was bursting with pride when Sir Robert Baden-Powell arrived. She showed him the camp.

Daisy's wish to live to see a World Camp in America had come true. She was sad, though, when they gathered around the campfire on the last evening for talks and farewells. At last they rose and in hushed voices sang taps:

"Day is done,
Gone the sun
From the lake,
From the hill,
From the sky.
All is well,
Safely rest
God is nigh."

Less than a year later, on January 17, 1927, Daisy Low died at her home in Savannah. But the spirit of Juliette Gordon Low still lives in the Girl Scout work she started.

Her birthplace in Savannah is preserved as a memorial. Thousands of girls from all over the world visit it. In 1927, the Juliette Low World Friendship Fund was established in her honor. The money is used to send Girl Scouts and Guides to camps and conferences all over the world. These are fine memorials to the woman who really had something wonderful *"for the girls of Savannah, and America, and all the world."*

3595